Hot Dogs

Across the USA

Discover the Hottest Hot Dog Recipes

BY

Christina Tosch

Copyright Notes

This Book may not be reproduced, in part or in whole, without explicit permission and agreement by the Author by any means. This includes but is not limited to print, electronic media, scanning, photocopying or file sharing.

The Author has made every effort to ensure accuracy of information in the Book but assumes no responsibility should personal or commercial damage arise in the case of misinterpretation or misunderstanding. All suggestions, instructions and guidelines expressed in the Book are meant for informational purposes only, and the Reader assumes any and all risk when following said information.

Table of Contents

Introduction

Chicago serves hot dogs with onion relish, pepper, tomato, mustard, pickle, and celery salt.

Coney Islanders prefer their hot dogs topped with chili, cheese, onions, and mustard. While the South loves slaws and chili topped hot dogs.

One thing is for sure though, while regional hot dog recipes vary from state to state, across the USA and beyond, Americans love a good hot dog.

Read on and discover some fascinating and frank facts about the humble hot dog.

- Every year on Independence Day, Americans tuck-into around 150 million hot dogs
- In 2014, a hot dog sold in Seattle, Washington for a staggering $169. It included foie gras, caviar, shaved black truffles, and Maitake mushrooms
- The next celebration of National Hot Dog Day falls on July 22nd, 2020
- Mustard is the No. 1 hot dog topping closely followed by ketchup
- The British royal family loves a good hot dog too. In 1939 when the King and Queen of England visited the Roosevelts in New York, they enjoyed a picnic, including hot dogs!
- Every year in July, the nation celebrates National Hot Dog Month

Hot Dogs from Across the USA brings together 40 of the hottest hot dog recipes ever!

Hot Dogs

Alaskan Hot Dogs with Cider and Caramelized Onions

Reindeer hot dogs are top of the go-to foods in Alaska. You can find them in gourmet food stores or online.

Servings: 4

Total Time: 30mins

Ingredients:

- 3 tbsp butter
- 1 Vidalia onion (peeled and sliced)
- Salt and black pepper
- ½ cup hard apple cider
- 4 reindeer hot dogs
- 4 hot dog buns (split and toasted)
- 4 dill pickle spears (to serve)
- Grainy mustard (to serve)

Directions:

1. Over moderate heat and in a skillet melt the butter.

2. Spreading the slices out add the onion to the skillet, and liberally season.

3. Cook while frequently stirring for 15 minutes until golden, beginning to caramelize and fork-tender.

4. Using the cider, deglaze the pan and cook for 5-10 minutes until the alcohol is cooked out, and the mixture has thickened. Keep the mixture warm.

5. In the meantime, cook the hot dogs on a grill until they are sufficiently cooked through in the middle and brown on the surface.

6. When you are ready to assemble the hot dogs, lay a cooked hot dog inside a toasted bun.

7. Top with cider onions, dill pickle, and mustard.

8. Serve and enjoy.

Baltimore Crab Mac 'n' Cheese Dog

Surf meets turf to create this cheesy hot dog snack.

Servings: 1

Total Time: 8mins

Ingredients:

- 1 hot dog
- 1 hot dog bun (split and toasted)
- 2 tbsp store-bought mac n' cheese (warmed)
- 4 ounces lump crab meat
- Old Bay seasoning (to taste)

Directions:

1. Cook the hot dog according to the package directions.

2. Toast the hot dog bun and warm through the store-bought mac n' cheese.

3. Place the hot dog inside the warm bun and top with warmed mac n' cheese followed by the crab meat.

4. Season to taste with Old Bay seasoning and enjoy.

Boston Fenway Frank

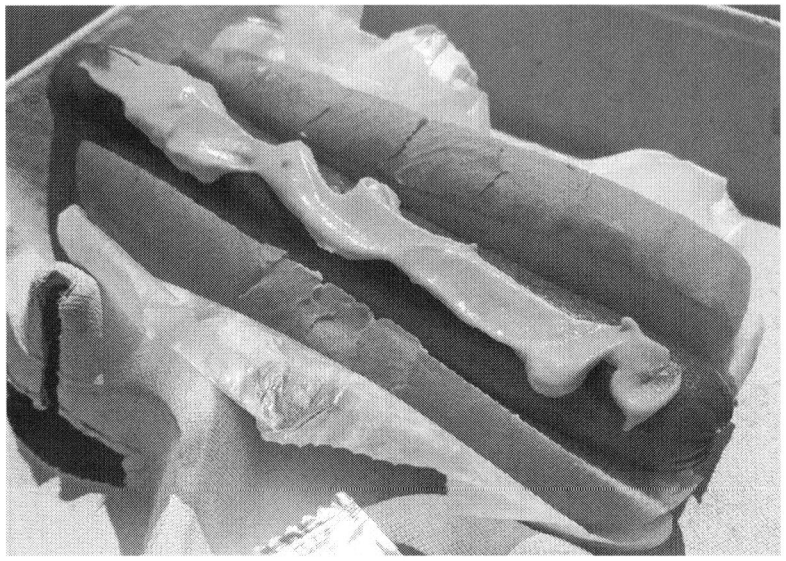

Baseball and the humble hot dog go hand in hand, and this simple snack pays homage to the Boston Red Sox and gets its name from their home at Fenway Park.

Servings: 1

Total Time: 10mins

Ingredients:

- 1 all-beef frank
- 1 hot dog bun (split and buttered on inside)
- 1 tbsp onion (peeled and finely chopped)
- 1 tbsp green sweet pickle relish
- 1 tsp yellow mustard

Directions:

1. Boil, steam, or grill the frank.

2. Grill the hot dog bun, cut side facing downwards.

3. Put the frank inside the bun and top with finely chopped onion, sweet pickle relish, and a generous squirt of yellow mustard.

4. Enjoy.

Buffalo Wing Hot Dogs

Two all-American favorites, buffalo wings, and hot dogs, combine to deliver a savory snack to remember.

Servings: 6

Total Time: 20mins

Ingredients:

- 6 hot dogs
- 6 hot dog buns (split and warmed)
- 1½ cups blue cheese (crumbled)
- ½ -1 cup store-bought buffalo wing sauce
- 1 bunch green onions

Directions:

1. Preheat the grill.

2. Grill the hot dogs under the grill until cooked to your preference.

3. Set your oven to low broil.

4. Put the cooked hot dogs inside the warmed buns and arrange on a baking sheet.

5. Add an equal amount of cheese on top of each hot dog and place in the oven. Broil for 3-5 minutes, until the cheese entirely melts.

6. Remove the baking sheet from the oven and drizzle the hot dogs with buffalo wing sauce.

7. Garnish with green onions and serve.

Cajun Andouille Dog

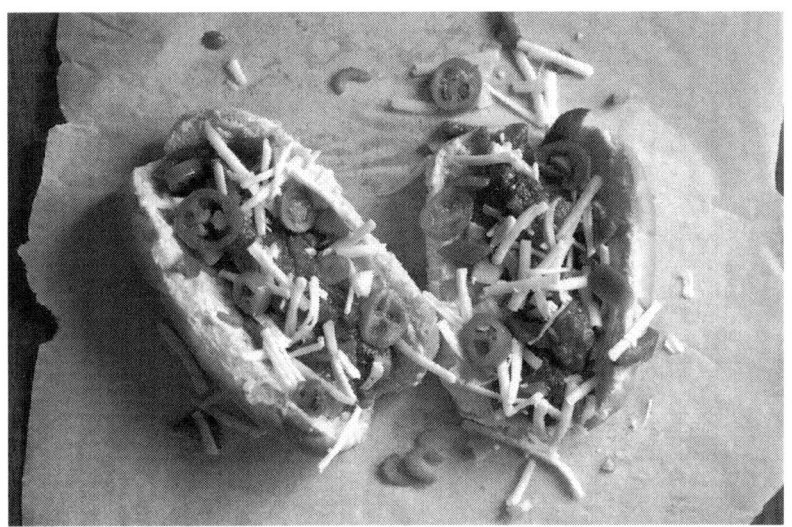

Hot dogs get a Southern makeover with this Louisiana-inspired recipe.

Servings: 4

Total Time: 35mins

Ingredients:

- 4 Andouille sausages
- 4 hot dog buns
- 1 cup celery (finely chopped)
- ½ cup green bell peppers (chopped)
- ½ cup roasted red bell pepper (chopped)
- ¼ cup Spanish red onion (peeled and chopped)
- 1 (12 ounce) jar pickled jalapeno slices
- 1 cup white Cheddar cheese (shredded)

Directions:

1. Preheat the grill.

2. Cook the sausages under the grill until sufficiently heated through. Remove, cover, and set aside to rest.

3. Split and toast the buns.

4. Divide the celery, green peppers, red bell peppers, red onion, and pickled jalapeno slices into 4 portions.

5. Put a sausage inside each bun and top with a portion of celery, green peppers, red bell peppers, red onion, and pickled jalapeno slices.

6. Top with shredded cheese and enjoy.

California Guacamole Dogs

You can rely on those wily Californians to come up with a health-conscious spin on the nation's favorite food, and this recipe is proof-positive that hot dogs needn't be packed full of unhealthy fats.

Servings: 8

Total Time: 15mins

Ingredients:

Guacamole:

- 1 Fresno chile (stem removed and discarded)
- 4 ripe, large-size avocados (peeled, pitted, and quartered)
- ½ cup red onion (peeled and minced)
- 1 tbsp freshly squeezed lime juice
- ½ tsp ground cumin
- ¼ tsp red chili flakes
- ½ tsp salt (to season)

Hot dogs:

- 8 turkey hot dogs
- 8 whole-grain hot dog buns
- Zesty guacamole (see recipe)

Directions:

1. For the guacamole: First, mince the chile and add to a bowl.

2. Add the avocado, onion, lime juice, cumin, chili flakes, and salt to the bowl and while making sure some large chunks of avocado remain, mash to combine

3. Arrange the hot dogs in a single layer on a preheated grill. Ideally, they should be approximately 4" away from the flame. Cook for between 6-10 minutes, until sufficiently cooked through.

4. Around 1 minute before the dogs are ready, split the buns open and warm on the grill.

5. Put the dogs inside the warmed buns and top with guacamole.

Chicago-Style Hot Dogs

The Windy City sure knows a thing or two about hot dogs, and this hot dog recipe certainly packs a punch.

Servings: 4

Total Time: 35mins

Ingredients:

- 4 large hot dog buns (split)
- 3 tbsp butter (melted)
- 1 tbsp poppy seeds
- 4 hot dogs
- 1 tbsp yellow mustard
- ¼ white onion (peeled and finely chopped)
- ¼ cup pickle relish
- 1 large-size tomato (sliced and cut into half moons)
- 4 dill pickles
- 8 sport peppers
- ½ tsp celery salt

Directions:

1. Preheat the main oven to 350 degrees F.

2. Lightly brush the outside of each bun with melted butter. Scatter poppy seeds over the top.

3. Arrange the buns, seam side facing downwards on a baking sheet.

4. Bake the bun for 10 minutes until toasted and the seeds are beginning to adhere to the bun.

5. In a deep pan of boiling water, boil the hot dogs until warm through. This will take approximately 5 minutes.

6. Put the hot dogs in the buns and top with yellow mustard, onion, pickle relish, slices of tomato, pickle spears, and peppers. Season with a pinch of celery salt.

7. Serve and enjoy.

Cincinnati Chili Dogs

Cocoa is the secret ingredient in this party-pleasing chili dog recipe.

Servings: 10

Total Time: 4hours 15mins

Ingredients:

- 1½ pounds ground beef
- 2 small yellow onions (peeled, chopped, and divided)
- 2 (15 ounce) cans tomato sauce
- 1½ tsp baking cocoa
- ½ tsp ground cinnamon
- ¼ tsp chili powder
- ¼ tsp paprika
- ¼ tsp garlic powder
- 2 tbsp Worcestershire sauce
- 1 tbsp cider vinegar
- 10 hot dogs
- 10 hot dog buns (split)
- Cheddar cheese (shredded)

Directions:

1. In a large frying pan over moderate heat, cook the beef, while stirring and using the back of a wooden spoon to break the meat up. Cook until no pink remains and drain.

2. In a slow cooker of 3-quart capacity, combine the beef with half of the chopped onions.

3. Add the tomato sauce, cocoa, cinnamon, chili powder, paprika, garlic powder, Worcestershire sauce, and vinegar. Cover and cook on low for approximately 2 hours.

4. Add the hot dogs to the slow cooker and continue to cook, while covered, on low for an additional 2 hours or until heated through.

5. Serve on the buns and top with shredded Cheddar and the remaining chopped onions.

6. Enjoy.

Cleveland Polish Boy

Although made with kielbasa, a Polish Boy is undoubtedly Cleveland's signature take on the ever-popular hot dog.

Servings: 2

Total Time: 15mins

Ingredients:

- 16 ounces frozen French fries
- 2 kielbasa links (cooked)
- ½ tbsp canola oil
- 2 hot dog buns (toasted)
- ¼ cup store-bought BBQ sauce (of choice)
- 1 cup store-bought slaw

Directions:

1. Cook the fries according to the package directions and until golden.

2. In the meantime, cook the kielbasa. Over moderate-high heat, heat a skillet.

3. Add the oil to the skillet and heat until it begins to shimmer.

4. Cook the kielbasa in the oil while frequently turning until sufficient cooked and heated through.

5. Put each link inside a toasted hot dog bun.

6. Evenly divide the BBQ sauce and spoon it over the kielbasa followed by the fries and finally the slaw.

7. Serve and enjoy.

Coney Island Hot Dogs

There are lots of different versions of what makes a good Coney Island hot dog, but whatever your point of view, this recipe is flavorful, perfectly spiced, and makes for a real show -stopping snack.

Servings: 8

Total Time: 1hour

Ingredients:

- 1 pound ground beef
- ½ cup yellow onion (peeled and diced)
- 2½ tbsp chili powder
- 1 tbsp cumin
- ½ tsp salt
- ½ tsp garlic powder
- ½ tsp celery salt
- 8 ounces tomato sauce
- ¼ cup water
- 1 tbsp yellow mustard
- 1 tbsp Worcestershire sauce
- 8 hot dog buns
- 8 hot dogs

Toppings:

- Cheddar cheese (shredded)
- Onion (peeled and finely diced)
- Yellow mustard (to serve)

Directions:

1. Over moderate-high heat, heat a large frying pan.

2. Add the beef along with the onion to the pan and cook, using the back of a wooden spoon to break the meat up as it cooks. Cook until the onion is soft, and the beef is browned.

3. Stir in the chili powder followed by the cumin, salt, garlic powder, and celery salt and cook for a few more minutes.

4. Stir in the tomato sauce, water, yellow mustard, and Worcestershire sauce. Bring the mixture to boil before reducing the heat and simmering for 20 minutes, until thickened. You may need to add a drop of water to loosen the consistency.

5. While the sauce is simmering preheat the main oven to 300 degrees F.

6. Wrap the hot dog buns in aluminum foil and transfer to the oven for 10 minutes, until warmed through.

7. Put the hot dogs in a large pan and pour in sufficient water to cover. Bring to boil and cook for 5-8 minutes, until heated through.

8. Put the hot dogs in the buns and top with the chili, shredded Cheddar, diced onion and a squirt of yellow mustard.

- Prep Time: 15 minutes
- Cook Time: 30 minutes
- Total Time: 45 minutes

Copycat Disney Corn Dogs

If you have ever been lucky enough to visit the Magic Kingdom in Orlando, Florida, then you know just how good these copycat corn dogs really are.

Servings: 8

Total Time: 35mins

Ingredients:

- ¾ cup cornmeal
- ¾ cup flour
- 1 tbsp sugar
- ⅓ tsp salt
- 1½ tsp baking powder
- 1 medium-size egg
- 1 tbsp cooking oil
- 2 tbsp honey
- ¾ cup buttermilk
- 8 hot dogs
- 2 cups oil (for frying)

Directions:

1. Add the cornmeal, flour, sugar, salt, and baking powder to a mixing bowl and mix until entirely combined.

2. In a separate container, add the egg followed by the cooking oil and honey, and stir well to beat the egg into the mixture.

3. Transfer the egg mixture to the flour/baking powder mixture.

4. Pour in the buttermilk and stir to combine, while taking care not to over-mix.

5. Put the batter to one side to rest while you prepare the hot dogs.

6. Warm a frying pan to moderate heat.

7. Add 1" of oil to the pan (approximately 2 cups).

8. Insert a wooden stick into the end of each hot dog, to come around ¾ of the way up the hot dog's middle.

9. Pour 2-3 scoops of the batter into a tall glass.

10. Dip each hot dog in the batter and roll to evenly cover.

11. Fry the battered hot dog for approximately 60 seconds before rotating it ⅓ of the way around. Continue to fry for another 60 seconds, before again rotating it ⅓ of the way around.

12. Continue until each corn dark is golden.

13. Serve and enjoy.

Cowboy Hot Dogs

Unleash your inner cowboy with these bisto dogs cooked slowly and to perfection on an outdoor wood-fired grill or camping stove.

Servings: 4

Total Time: 30mins

Ingredients:

- 1 large-size yellow onion (peeled and cut into half-moons)
- 1 tbsp olive oil
- 4 bison dogs
- 4 hot dog buns (split)
- 6 tbsp mayonnaise
- 2 tbsp spicy brown mustard
- 4 tbsp BBQ sauce
- ½ cup white Cheddar cheese (shredded)
- 6 slices cooked bacon (crumbled)

Directions:

1. Over moderate heat in a large frying pan on an outdoor wood-fired grill or camping stove cook the onion in oil until golden and fork-tender. This will take between 15-20 minutes.

2. Grill the bison dogs until just charred all over, for approximately 5-6 minutes, while occasionally stirring.

3. Place the buns under the grill and while frequently turning, grill for 3 minutes, until warmed and slightly charred.

4. Spread mayonnaise over the insides of each bun and add a dollop of mustard and BBQ sauce.

5. Put the dogs inside the buns, and garnish with cheese, caramelized onions, and crumbled bacon.

6. Serve and enjoy.

Crock Pot Michigan Hot Dogs

A Michigan hot dog is a steamed hot dog served inside a steamed bun and loaded with a meaty Michigan tomato-based sauce. This Northern New York regional favorite is sure to quickly become your go-to topping, too.

Servings:-8

Total Time: 2hours 25mins

Ingredients

- 1 (15 ounce) can tomato sauce
- 4 tsp chili powder
- 2 tsp cumin powder
- 2 tsp garlic powder
- 2 tsp ground black pepper
- 2 tsp dried onion flakes
- 2 tsp crushed red pepper flakes
- ¼ tsp hot sauce
- 2 pounds lean ground beef
- 8 hot dogs (steamed)
- 9 hot dog buns (split and steamed)
- Onions (chopped, to serve)
- Yellow mustard (to serve)

Directions:

1. In a bowl, combine the tomato sauce with the chili powder, cumin powder, garlic powder, black pepper, onion flakes, red pepper flakes, and hot sauce. Stir to combine.

2. Add the ground beef to the bowl and mix as if you would when making meatballs.

3. Transfer the mixture to a crockpot and on low, cook for 2-4 hours.

4. Once the meat is sufficiently cooked through, break it up to a chunk-free, very fine consistency using the back of a wooden spoon. Set aside until you are ready to serve.

5. Steam the hot dogs along with the dog buns.

6. Serve the meat inside the hot dog buns, top with chopped onions and a squirt of yellow mustard.

Georgia Peach Hot Dogs

What better way to celebrate The Peach State of Georgia than with this sweet and savory hot dog recipe which features a homemade fruity relish.

Servings: 2

Total Time: 1hour 5mins

Ingredients:

Peach Relish:

- Olive oil
- ½ pound red onion (peeled and diced)
- 1 tsp red chili flakes
- 3 tbsp whole-grain mustard
- ⅓ cup honey
- ¼ cup red wine vinegar
- ¼ tsp salt
- ½ tsp freshly ground black pepper
- 3 cups ripe peaches (peeled, pitted, and diced)

Hot Dogs:

- 2 hot dogs
- 2 hot dog buns
- 2 tbsp toasted pecans (chopped)

Directions:

1. First, prepare the relish. In a pan, heat the olive oil.

2. Add the onions to the pan and over moderate heat, sauté for 5-7 minutes, until tender and mostly translucent. Add the chili flakes to the pan and cook for between 1-2 minutes.

3. Next, stir in the mustard and cook for 1-2 minutes to combine.

4. Add the honey followed by the vinegar, stirring to incorporate — season with salt and black pepper.

5. Add the peaches, stirring to combine.

6. Bring the ingredients to boil before reducing the heat to a medium simmer. Cook until the majority of the liquid has cooked off, and the remaining liquid is a thick, syrup-like consistency. This will take between 35-40 minutes over moderate-low heat.

7. Season to taste and transfer to the fridge to chill until you are ready to serve.

8. For the hot dogs: Grill the sausage dogs under the grill until crisp on the outside and cooked through.

9. Warm the buns under the grill.

10. Put the hot dogs in the buns and top with relish.

11. Garnish with pecans and serve.

12. Summertime Hot Dog Challenge - Home & Family

Hawaiian-Style Hot Dogs with Grilled Pineapple and Teriyaki Mayonnaise

Embrace a taste of the tropics with these Hawaiian-style hot dogs topped with juicy grilled pineapple and served with a homemade teriyaki mayonnaise.

Servings: 8

Total Time: 20mins

Ingredients:

- Oil

Teriyaki Mayo:

- ¼ cup real mayonnaise
- 3 tbsp teriyaki sauce
- ½ tbsp freshly squeezed lime juice
- Pinch of sea salt

Hot Dogs:

- ½ fresh pineapple (halved and sliced)
- 1 tsp grapeseed oil
- ½ tsp cayenne pepper
- 8 hot dogs
- 8 hot dog buns

Directions:

1. Preheat your grill to high heat and lightly oil the grill grate.

2. In a bowl, combine the mayonnaise with the teriyaki sauce, fresh lime juice, and pinch of sea salt. Mix to incorporate.

3. In a second bowl, toss the slices of pineapple along with the grapeseed oil before grilling until grill marks appear, for 2 minutes. Flip the slices of pineapple over and season with cayenne pepper. Remove the pineapple from the grill.

4. Reduce the grill heat down to moderate-high and grill the hot dogs until cooked through, and flipping over a couple of times, for 8-10 minutes.

5. Lightly toast the hot dog buns for 60 seconds.

6. Put the hot dogs in the buns and top with grilled pineapple, teriyaki mayo, and your favorites toppings.

Hot Dogs Waco Style

Planning a movie night in? Grab the remote, pull up a chair, and enjoy these juice hot dogs with a cold beer.

Servings: 2

Total Time: 12mins

Ingredients:

- 4 all-beef hot dogs
- 4 large-size hot dog buns
- 4-6 rashers of bacon (fried and crumbled)
- ½ cup sweet onion (peeled and chopped)
- ½ cup mature cheddar cheese (shredded)
- ½ cup Roma tomatoes (diced)
- BBQ sauce (to taste)
- Jalapeno pepper (seeded and diced)

Directions:

1. Under a hot grill, cook the hot dogs to your preferred level of doneness.

2. Toast the hot dog buns.

3. Put the hot dogs inside the buns and layer the remaining ingredients on top (crumbled bacon, onion, Cheddar cheese, diced tomatoes, BBQ sauce, and diced jalapeno peppers.

4. Enjoy.

Hot Dogs with Pennsylvania Greek Sauce

Contrary to its name, Greek sauce is a western Pennsylvania regional favorite. It's the perfect topping for hamburgers, French fries, and hot dogs.

Servings: 8

Total Time: 1hour

Ingredients:

- 1 pound ground beef
- 2 small onions (peeled and chopped)
- 1 (8 ounce) can tomato sauce
- 1 cup water
- ½ tsp salt
- ½ tsp black pepper
- ½ tsp each dried basil, oregano, cumin, and garlic powder
- 2 tsp yellow mustard
- 1 tsp red pepper flakes (crushed)
- 8 hot dogs
- 8 hot dog buns

Directions:

1. Over moderate heat, cook the beef in a large frying pan until entirely brown. Drain.

2. Stir the onions followed by the tomato sauce, water, salt, black pepper, basil, oregano, cumin, garlic powder, yellow mustard, and red pepper flakes into the browned beef.

3. Bring the mixture to boil before reducing the heat to moderate-low and simmer while occasionally stirring for 45 minutes.

4. Cook the hot dogs according to your preferred level of doneness and toast the hot dog buns.

5. Put the hot dogs inside the buns and top with the Greek sauce.

6. Enjoy.

Independence Day Beer-Soaked Hot Dogs

Every year, on July 4th, Americans consume 150 million hot dogs! So, tuck-in and enjoy.

Servings: 8

Total Time: 30mins

Ingredients:

- 8 beef hot dogs
- 1 (12 ounce) bottle beer (of choice)
- 1 large-size white onion (peeled, cut in half, and sliced)
- 1 red pepper (sliced into strips)
- 1 green pepper (sliced into strips)
- 8 strips bacon (chopped)
- 1 pound mushrooms (sliced)
- 2 cloves garlic (peeled and minced)
- Extra- virgin olive oil
- Salt and freshly ground black pepper
- 8 hot dog buns

Optional Toppings:

- Cheese (grated)
- Avocado (peeled, pitted, and sliced)
- Jalapeno (sliced)
- Ketchup and mustard (to serve)

Directions:

1. On an angle, cut small slits into each hot dog approximately ½" deep.

2. Put the hot dogs in a large cup and add the beer. Allow to marinate for a minimum of half an hour.

3. To assemble the foil packets. Take 2 large size pieces of heavy aluminum foil.

4. To one, add the onions along with the red and green peppers.

5. To the second, add bacon, mushrooms, and garlic.

6. Drizzle olive oil over both and season with salt and freshly ground pepper.

7. Fold the short ends together and fold to entirely seal. Fold in the sides to seal while allowing room to steam.

8. Preheat your grill to moderate-high heat.

9. Arrange the hot dogs and packets on the grill, and grill the dogs for 5-10 minutes, until pleasantly charred and the slits open up.

10. Cook the packets for approximately 20 minutes, moving to the middle of the grill once the dogs are cooked through and increasing the heat to high.

11. Assemble the hot dogs with the hot dog buns and preferred toppings.

Indiana-Style Corn Dogs

Indiana always has a reason to party, and over the year, there are lots of festival and State Fairs, and what better finger food is there to enjoy during these occasions than a tasty corn dog.

Servings: 12

Total Time: 30mins

Ingredients:

- 1 cup all-purpose flour
- ½ cup yellow cornmeal
- 1 tbsp sugar
- 3 tsp baking powder
- 1 tsp salt
- ½ tsp ground mustard
- ¼ tsp paprika
- Dash of black pepper
- 1 large egg (lightly beaten)
- 1 cup evaporated milk
- Oil (to fry)
- 12 hot dogs

Directions:

1. In a mixing bowl, whisk the flour with the cornmeal, sugar, baking powder, salt, mustard, paprika, and black pepper.

2. Whisk in the egg and evaporated milk until blended.

3. Transfer the batter mixture to a tall glass.

4. In a deep-fat fryer or electric skillet and heat the oil to 375 degrees F.

5. Insert the skewers into the hot dogs.

6. Dip the hot dogs into the batter, allowing any excess to drip off.

7. In batches, fry the corn dogs until golden brown, for 2-3 minutes, while occasionally turning.

8. Drain the dogs on kitchen paper towel and serve.

Kansas City Dogs

A cookout isn't a cookout without good ole American hot dogs. So, pop these dogs on your outdoor charcoal or gas grill, and in no time at all, you and your friends will be tucking into a meal worthy of the Sunflower or Wheat State of Kansas. Enjoy!

Servings: 8

Total Time: 15mins

Ingredients:

- 8 beef hot dogs
- 1 cup store-bought BBQ pulled pork
- 8 hot dog buns (split)
- 2 tbsp medium green onions
- ½ cup pickle slices
- Mustard (to serve)
- 8 hot dog buns (split)

Directions:

1. Preheat your charcoal or gas grill.

2. Arrange the hot dogs on the grill over moderate heat and uncovered, cook for between 10-15 minutes while frequently turning until heated through.

3. Add the pulled pork to a microwave-safe bowl, partially cover and on high, microwave for 45-60 seconds, while stirring every 30 seconds. When sufficiently heated through, remove from the microwave.

4. Put the hot dogs in the buns and top each with approximately 2 tbsp of pulled pork.

5. Garnish with onions, pickles, and a squirt of mustard.

Mac 'n Cheese Dogs

Two iconic American foods come together to deliver the perfect meal for all the family to enjoy.

Servings: 4

Total Time: 20mins

Ingredients:

- 2 tbsp butter
- 2 tbsp all-purpose flour
- 2 cups milk
- Kosher salt
- Freshly ground black pepper
- 2 cups Cheddar cheese (shredded)
- 1 pound macaroni elbow (cooked, drained, keep warm)
- 4 hot dogs
- 4 hot dog buns (split)
- 6 rashers of bacon (cooked and crumbled)
- Fresh chives (chopped, to garnish)

Directions:

1. Over moderate heat, and in a large frying pan, melt the butter.

2. Add the flour to the pan and whisk until entirely combined. Cook for 60 seconds, until golden.

3. Pour in the milk and season.

4. Allow the mixture to thicken for a few minutes before adding the shredded Cheddar cheese. Stir until the cheese melts before adding the drained pasta and stirring until well and evenly coated.

5. Grill or boil the hot dogs to your preferred level of doneness.

6. Put the hot dogs inside the hot dog buns and top with Mac n' cheese, crumbled bacon, and chopped chives.

Nebraska Cornhusker Hot Dog

This hot dog pays homage to the Nebraska Cornhuskers football team. So if you are a football fan, get cooking!

Servings: 6

Total Time: 15mins

Ingredients:

- 6 all-beef hot dogs
- 6 hot dog buns
- 12 slices of Provolone cheese
- Tomato corn relish (as needed)
- Corn chips (as needed)

Directions:

1. Boil or grill the hot dogs to your preferred doneness.

2. Toast the buns.

3. Arrange 2 slices of cheese inside each hot dog bun and top with a hot dog, garnish with tomato corn relish, and corn chips.

4. Enjoy.

New Jersey Italian Hot Dog

You will certainly need a big appetite to polish off one of these hot dogs. The filling is so generous you will need to source very large sandwich buns.

Servings: 4

Total Time: 40mins

Ingredients:

- ¼ cup extra-virgin olive oil
- 2 pounds potatoes (peeled and cut into ½" chunks)
- Salt
- 2 red bell peppers (sliced into strips)
- 1 large yellow onion (peeled and cut into strips)
- 1 tsp Italian seasoning
- 8 beef hot dogs
- 4 sandwich or large hot dog buns*
- Mustard (to serve)

Directions:

1. First, fry the potatoes by heating the oil in a large skillet until it begins to shimmer.

2. In a single layer, fry the potatoes on moderate-high heat for 2-3 minutes. Do not stir or touch the potatoes.

3. With a metal spatula scrape the potatoes off the bottom of the pan, flipping them over during cooking.

4. Season the potatoes with salt and cook for an additional few minutes, again without touching.

5. Remove the potatoes from the pan and set them aside in a bowl.

6. Increase the heat to high and add the red and peppers along with the onion.

7. Distribute the veggies evenly in the pan and cook, without touching, for 2-3 minutes.

8. Season with salt and flip over, cooking for an additional 2-3 minutes. Some bits will be blackened and browned.

9. Sprinkle in the Italian seasoning and add the potatoes to the pan, stirring to combine and cooking over moderate-high heat until browned and fork-tender for 8-10 minutes.

10. Heat a frying pan or grill and cook the hot dogs to your preferred level of doneness and put to one side.

11. To assemble: Generously spread the mustard on both sides of the rolls.

12. Put 2 hot dogs into each roll and pile with potatoes, peppers, and onions.

13. Serve and enjoy.

*You will need exceptionally large buns to accommodate all the fillings!

Peanut Butter and Bacon Hot Dog

Forget PB&J and instead opt for PB&B hot dogs!

Servings: 4

Total Time: 25mins

Ingredients:

- 4 rashers bacon
- 4 all-beef hot dogs
- 4 hot dog buns (split)
- ¼ cup mayonnaise
- ½ cup smooth peanut butter
- 1 shallot (thinly sliced)
- ½ cup cheese (shredded)

Directions:

1. Cook the bacon in a skillet until cooked through and crisp. Remove from the skillet and set aside to drain and cool on a paper towel-lined plate. Chop into small pieces.

2. Preheat your grill and cook the hot dogs.

3. Toast the buns and spread the cut side of each bun with mayonnaise.

4. Put a hot dog inside each bun and top with peanut butter, shallots, bacon, and shredded cheese.

5. Enjoy.

Philly Cheese Steak Dog

Hot dogs topped with a juicy East Coast-style Philly cheesesteak have to be the best game-night in treat ever!

Servings: 8

Total Time: 25mins

Ingredients:

- 1 tbsp olive oil
- ½ large-size onion (peeled and diced)
- ½ pound shaved rib-eye (chopped)
- 8 hot dogs
- 8 hot dog buns (split)
- 8 ounces processed cheese spread

Directions:

1. Over moderate heat, in a skillet, heat the oil.

2. Add the onion to the hot oil and while stirring cook until tender for between 5-10 minutes. Transfer the cooked onion to a bowl.

3. Using the same skillet, cook the rib eye for 5-10 minutes until the meat has no pink remaining, and the liquid is evaporated.

4. Return the onion to the skillet.

5. Bring a pan filled with water to boil.

6. Add the hot dogs to the boiling water and cook for 5-10 minutes.

7. Put a cooked hot dog inside each hot dog bun.

8. Spoon the rib eye-onion mixture over the hot dogs and top with processed cheese spread.

Pretzel Dogs

Pretzel dogs lightly brushed with garlic butter and parsley and baked until golden brown in the oven are simply delicious.

Servings: 4

Total Time: 35mins

Ingredients:

- Flour (to dust)
- 12 ounces pizza dough
- 4 hot dogs
- ¼ cup baking soda
- 5 cups water
- 1 egg yolk (beaten)
- 2 tbsp butter (melted)
- 2 cloves garlic (peeled and minced)
- 1 tbsp fresh parsley (chopped)

Directions:

1. Preheat the main oven to 450 degrees F.

2. Lightly dust a chopping board with flour.

3. Cut the pizza dough into 4 equal-sized portions.

4. Roll each portion of dough out to a 12" rope.

5. Wrap the dough rope around a hot dog in a spiral fashion, leaving room on each end.

6. In a pan, combine the baking soda together with the water and bring to boil.

7. Cook each wrapped hot dog in the baking soda solution for 30 seconds. Using a slotted spoon, take the hot dog out of the mixture and place on a baking tray.

8. Lightly brush each pretzel hot dog with the beaten eggs.

9. In a bowl, combine the melted butter with the minced garlic and parsley and brush over the top.

10. Bake in the oven until the pretzel dogs are golden brown, for 12-15 minutes.

11. Enjoy.

Reuben Hot Dogs

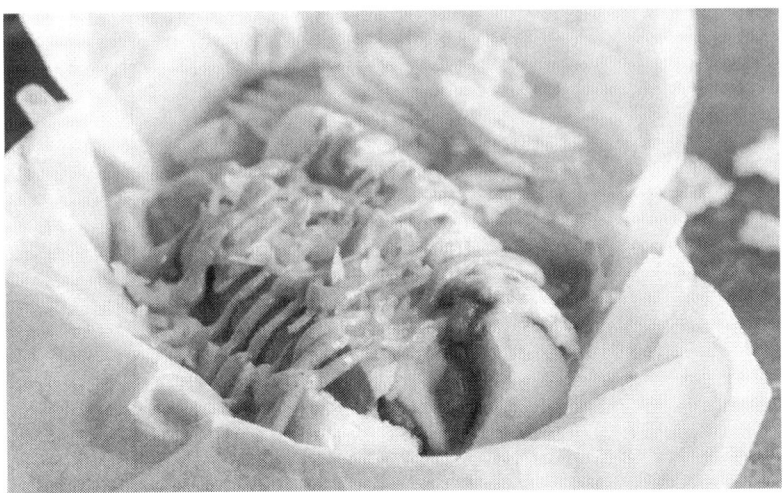

A classic Reuben sandwich gets a hot dog makeover. Can a frankfurter get any more fantastic?

Servings: 8

Total Time: 15mins

Ingredients:

- 8 classic hot dog franks
- 8 thin slices pastrami
- 8 hot dog buns
- 8 slices Swiss cheese
- 1 cup store-bought sauerkraut (warmed)
- 8 tsp Thousand Island dressing

Directions:

1. Cook the hot dogs to your preferred level of doneness using your favorite method of cooking.

2. Add 1 slice of pastrami to each bun.

3. Put a hot dog on top of the pastrami, followed by a slice of cheese and 2 tablespoons of sauerkraut.

4. Drizzle with Thousand Island dressing and serve.

Print

Rhode Island Hot Wieners

The hot wiener, or New York System wiener, a quintessential part of the food culture of Rhode Island.

Servings: 8

Total Time: 55mins

Ingredients:

- ¼ cup butter (cubed)
- 1 medium-size onion (peeled and finely chopped)
- 2 tbsp Worcestershire sauce
- 2 tbsp paprika
- 2 tbsp chili powder
- 3 tsp ground cumin
- 1 tsp ground mustard
- ¾ tsp ground cinnamon
- ½ tsp ground allspice
- 1 pound ground beef
- ¼ cup water
- 8 hot dog buns
- 8 hot dogs (cooked)

Toppings:

- Yellow mustard
- Onion (peeled and finely chopped)
- Celery salt

Directions:

1. In a large frying pan over moderate heat, melt the butter.

2. Add the onion to the pan and cook while stirring until fork tender, for 3-4 minutes.

3. Stir in the Worcestershire sauce along with the paprika, chili powder, ground cumin, ground mustard, ground cinnamon, and ground allspice.

4. Add the beef to the pan and cook while breaking the meat up with the back of a wooden spoon for 6-8 minutes, or until no pink remains.

5. Pour in the water and stir. Bring to boil before reducing the heat and simmering, while uncovered for half an hour.

6. Finally, steam the hot dog buns. Fill the bottom section of a double boiler with cold water and place it on your stovetop over high heat. Bring to water. Add the buns to the top section of the double boiler and position it on top of the now boiling water. Cover with a lid and steam the buns for a couple of minutes. Using kitchen tongs, take the lid off and remove the buns.

7. Put the hot dogs inside the buns, and top with the meat sauce, a squirt of mustard, and a sprinkling of onion and celery salt.

San Francisco Bay Dog

Farmer's markets and fresh produce are in abundance in the beautiful Bay Area, and this gourmet hot dog served with homemade mayonnaise, and a crisp salad provides the perfect showcase for everything this area has to offer.

Servings: 8

Total Time: 18mins

Ingredients:

Mayonnaise:

- ½ cup mayonnaise
- ¼ cup mixed fresh herbs* (finely chopped)

Salad:

- 4 radishes (trimmed)
- 2 small Persian cucumbers
- 1 large-size carrot (peeled)
- 2 tbsp virgin olive oil
- 1 tbsp rice wine vinegar
- Salt and freshly ground black pepper

Hot Dogs:

- 8 hot dogs
- 8 hot dog buns (split and toasted)
- ¼ cup fresh mint leaves (to serve)
- ¼ cup fresh cilantro leaves (to serve)

Directions:

1. For the mayonnaise: In a bowl, combine the mayo with the mixed herbs until entirely combined. Transfer to the fridge, tightly wrapped until you are ready to serve.

2. For the salad: First, using a mandolin thinly slice the radishes and place in a mixing bowl.

3. Again with the mandolin, slice the cucumbers and carrot very thinly lengthwise and add to the bowl of radishes.

4. Toss the veggies in the olive oil and rice wine vinegar to coat — season to taste.

5. For the hot dogs: Grill the dogs to your preferred level of doneness.

6. Spread a dollop of the herb mayonnaise onto the cut sides of each toasted bun.

7. Put a hot dog inside each bun and top with the cucumber, carrot, and radish salad.

8. Garnish with mint and cilantro leaves and serve.

*Cook's Note:

Basil, chives, cilantro, mint, parsley, and tarragon are all great choices

Santa Fe Dogs

New Mexico is famous for its green and red chile sauces. When both are served together in one dish, the colorful combination is called "Christmas."

Servings: 8

Total Time: 1hour 15mins

Ingredients:

Red Chile Sauce:

- 2 tbsp vegetable oil
- 1 onion (peeled and finely chopped)
- 2 garlic cloves (peeled and minced)
- ¾ cup ground red Chimayo chile
- 4 cups water
- 1 tsp dried oregano
- 1 tsp salt

Green Chile Sauce:

- 2 tbsp canola oil
- 1 onion (peeled and finely chopped)
- 2 garlic cloves (peeled and minced)
- 1 tsp ground cumin
- 1 tbsp flour
- 2 cups chopped roasted green chile
- 2 cups chicken stock
- 1 tsp salt

Hot Dogs:

- 8 hot dogs
- 8 hot dog buns (split and toasted)
- Pepper Jack Cheese (shredded)
- 1 onion (peeled and finely chopped)

Directions:

1. To prepare the red chile sauce: Over moderate heat, in a pan, heat the oil along with the onion and garlic and cook while occasionally stirring for approximately 8 minutes, until softened.

2. Stir in the red chile and slowly pour in the water while continually stirring.

3. Add the oregano along with the salt and bring to boil.

4. Turn the heat down to low and simmer for 20-25 minutes, until the sauce easily coats the back of a spoon.

5. For the green chile sauce: Over moderate heat, in a pan, heat the oil.

6. Add the onions to the pan and, while occasionally stirring, cook for 10 minutes, until softened.

7. Next, add the garlic followed by the cumin and cook for 30 seconds, until fragrant.

8. Add the flour and while constantly stirring cook for 60 seconds.

9. Add the green chile, followed by the stock and salt and bring to boil.

10. Turn the heat down to a simmer and cook while occasionally stirring until slightly thickened for approximately 15 minutes.

11. For the hot dogs: Grill the hot dogs to your preferred level of doneness.

12. Put the hot dog in the toasted hot dog buns.

13. Spoon the red and green chile sauces over the top.

14. Sprinkle with shredded Pepper Jack cheese and chopped onion.

15. Serve and enjoy.

Seattle Cream Cheese Dogs

This hot dog featuring warmed cream cheese and onions are often sold in Seattle on game day or from late-night food carts. Here, you can recreate this simple recipe at home.

Servings: 4

Total Time: 30mins

Ingredients:

- ¼ cup butter
- 1 sweet onion (peeled and thinly sliced)
- 4 ounces cream cheese
- 4 hot dogs
- Brown mustard
- Sauerkraut (to serve)

Directions:

1. Preheat the grill to moderate-high heat.

2. In a skillet over moderate heat, melt the butter. Add the onions to the pan and slowly cook for 15 minutes until they have softened and become a deep brown color.

3. In a small pan, warm the cream cheese over low heat until very soft.

4. Grill the hot dogs until browned, and lightly grill the buns on both sides.

5. To assemble the hot dogs, evenly spread the warmed cream cheese on the toasted bun. Put the hot dog inside the buns and top with sweet onions, brown mustard, and sauerkraut.

Sonoran Hot Dogs

Popular in the Mexican state of Sonora, as well as Tuscon and Phoenix in Arizona, this hog dog wrapped in mesquite-smoked bacon, originated in Sonora's capital, Hermosillo.

Servings: 8

Total Time: 30mins

Ingredients:

- 8 rashers of bacon
- 8 all-beef hot dogs
- 1 (15 ounce) can pinto beans (drained and rinsed)
- 1 tbsp butter
- 1 tsp ground cumin
- 1 tsp brown sugar
- Pinch of salt
- Dash of pepper
- 1 cup sour cream
- Freshly squeezed juice of 1 fresh lime
- 8 hot dog buns
- 2 medium tomatoes (diced)
- 1 white onion (peeled and minced)
- 8 ounces queso fresco (crumbled)
- Green tomatillo salsa
- Pickled jalapeños
- Fresh cilantro

Directions:

1. To prepare the hot dogs, take a rasher of bacon and wrap it tightly around the hot dog. Put it ends downwards on a plate; this will help to keep the hot dog firmly wrapped.

2. Preheat your grill to moderate-high heat. Add the hot dogs, ends facing downwards, and grill for approximately 10 minutes, while occasionally turning until the bacon is crisp and sufficiently cooked through.

3. Add the beans to a pot along with the butter, cumin, brown sugar, and a pinch of salt and a dash of pepper. Warm the beans through and keep warm.

4. In a bowl, combine the sour cream with the fresh lime juice to create a creamy sauce.

5. To assemble the dogs, put a bacon-wrapped hot dog inside a hot dog bun, top with warm pinto beans, tomatoes, onion, crumbled queso fresco, sour cream sauce, salsa, pickled jalapenos, and fresh cilantro.

St Patrick's Day Dogs

In a number of states in the USA, March 17th is an important date in the Irish-American calendar, and these dogs are perfect for this special day.

Servings: 8

Total Time: 25mins

Ingredients:

- 1 tsp butter
- ½ yellow onion (peeled and chopped)
- 1 (12 ounce) bottle Irish stout beer
- ½ cup butter
- 1 tsp garlic powder
- ½ tsp store-bought hot sauce
- 8 hot dogs
- 8 hot dog buns (split)

Directions:

1. Over moderate heat, in a skillet heat the 1 teaspoon butter.

2. Add the onion to the melted butter and cook while stirring until the onion softens and releases its liquid; this will take 8-10 minutes.

3. Pour in the beer and add the ½ cup butter followed by the garlic powder and hot sauce. Bring the mixture to boil until the stout is frothy.

4. Turn the heat down and add the hot dogs to the skillet, simmer for 5-8 minutes until the dogs are heated through.

5. Serve in hot dog buns and enjoy.

Tennessee Smoky Hot Dog

Those Southerners certainly know a thing or two about outdoor grilling, and these smoky hot dogs will get everyone gathering around the BBQ.

Servings: 8

Total Time: 45mins

Ingredients:

- 1 large-size sweet onion (peeled and cut into ¼" slices)
- 2 tbsp butter (divided)
- ¼ tsp BBQ rub (of choice)
- 2 cups store-bought hot dog chili
- 8 all-beef hot dogs
- 8 hot dog buns
- Yellow mustard (to serve)

Dressing:

- ½ cup mayonnaise
- 2 tbsp cider vinegar
- 1 tsp freshly ground black pepper
- 1 tsp kosher salt
- ½ tsp celery seed

Smoky Slaw:

- ¼ head purple cabbage (cut into 2 wedges)
- ½ head green cabbage (cut into 4 wedges)
- Olive oil
- 1 large carrot (peeled and shredded)
- ¼ cup sweet onion (peeled and diced)

Directions:

1. Preheat your charcoal grill for direct heat to a temperature of between 400-425 degrees F.

2. Arrange the slices of onion on top of a piece of heavy-duty foil.

3. Top with 1 tsp butter and season with the BBQ rub.

4. Fold the edges of the aluminum foil over and seal to create an envelope.

5. In a bowl, combine the dressing ingredients (mayonnaise, cider vinegar, black pepper, kosher salt, and celery seed. Mix well to entirely combine and transfer to the fridge until needed.

6. Put the foil pack on the grill. Add the hot dog chili to a pot and place that on the grill also. Cook both for approximately 10-15 minutes. You will need to flip the foil parcel over halfway through cooking.

7. In the meantime, prepare the slaw. Lightly brush the cut sides of the purple and green cabbage with olive oil and grill until lightly charred, for 3-4 minutes on each side. Remove the cabbage and set aside to cool.

8. Slice the cabbage wedges into matchsticks and add the carrot, onion, and prepared dressing to a large-size bowl and toss to coat evenly. Transfer to the refrigerator.

9. Grill the hot dogs to your preferred level of doneness, flipping over to ensure they are evenly cooked.

10. Remove all the food from the grill and assemble.

11. Put the hot dogs in the buns and top with onion, slaw, chili, and mustard.

12. Enjoy.

Thanksgiving Cheese Dogs

Inspired by a popular TV program featuring Mandy Moore, these cheesy dogs are worth coming home to!

Servings: 6

Total Time: 12mins

Ingredients:

- 6 hot dogs
- 6 single cheese slices
- 20 saltine crackers (crushed)

Directions:

1. Roast the hot dogs in the main oven at 350 degrees F until crisp and blistered.

2. Remove from the oven and skewer onto popsicle sticks.

3. While still hot, wrap a cheese slice around each hot dog, carefully pressing the edges together to seal.

4. Roll the wrapped dogs in the crushed crackers and serve at once.

Author's Afterthoughts

thank you

I would like to express my deepest thanks to you, the reader, for making this investment in one my books. I cherish the thought of bringing the love of cooking into your home.

With so much choice out there, I am grateful you decided to Purch this book and read it from beginning to end.

Please let me know by submitting an Amazon review if you enjoyed this book and found it contained valuable information to help you in your culinary endeavors. Please take a few minutes to express your opinion freely and honestly. This will help others make an informed decision on purchasing and provide me with valuable feedback.

Thank you for taking the time to review!

Christina Tosch

About the Author

Christina Tosch is a successful chef and renowned cookbook author from Long Grove, Illinois. She majored in Liberal Arts at Trinity International University and decided to pursue her passion of cooking when she applied to the world renowned Le Cordon Bleu culinary school in Paris, France. The school was lucky to recognize the immense talent of this chef and she excelled in her courses, particularly Haute Cuisine. This skill was recognized and rewarded by several highly regarded Chicago restaurants, where she was offered the prestigious position of head chef.

Christina and her family live in a spacious home in the Chicago area and she loves to grow her own vegetables and herbs in the garden she lovingly cultivates on her sprawling estate. Her and her husband have two beautiful children, 3 cats, 2 dogs and a parakeet they call Jasper. When Christina is not hard at work creating beautiful meals for Chicago's elite, she is hard at work writing engaging e-books of which she has sold over 1500.

Make sure to keep an eye out for her latest books that offer helpful tips, clear instructions and witty anecdotes that will bring a smile to your face as you read!

Printed in Great Britain
by Amazon

43497277R00071